AF444152

Plečnik Projects: Mapping the Embankments Along the Gradaščica and Ljubljanica

Kerry O'Connor

The research for this book was supported by a grant from the Architectural League of New York Deborah D. Norden Fund.

Published by O'Connor Architecture, PLLC

ISBN 979-8-218-11179-3

5   Introduction

9   The Section of Water

21 Ljubljanica River

31 Gradaščica River

43 Index of Conditions

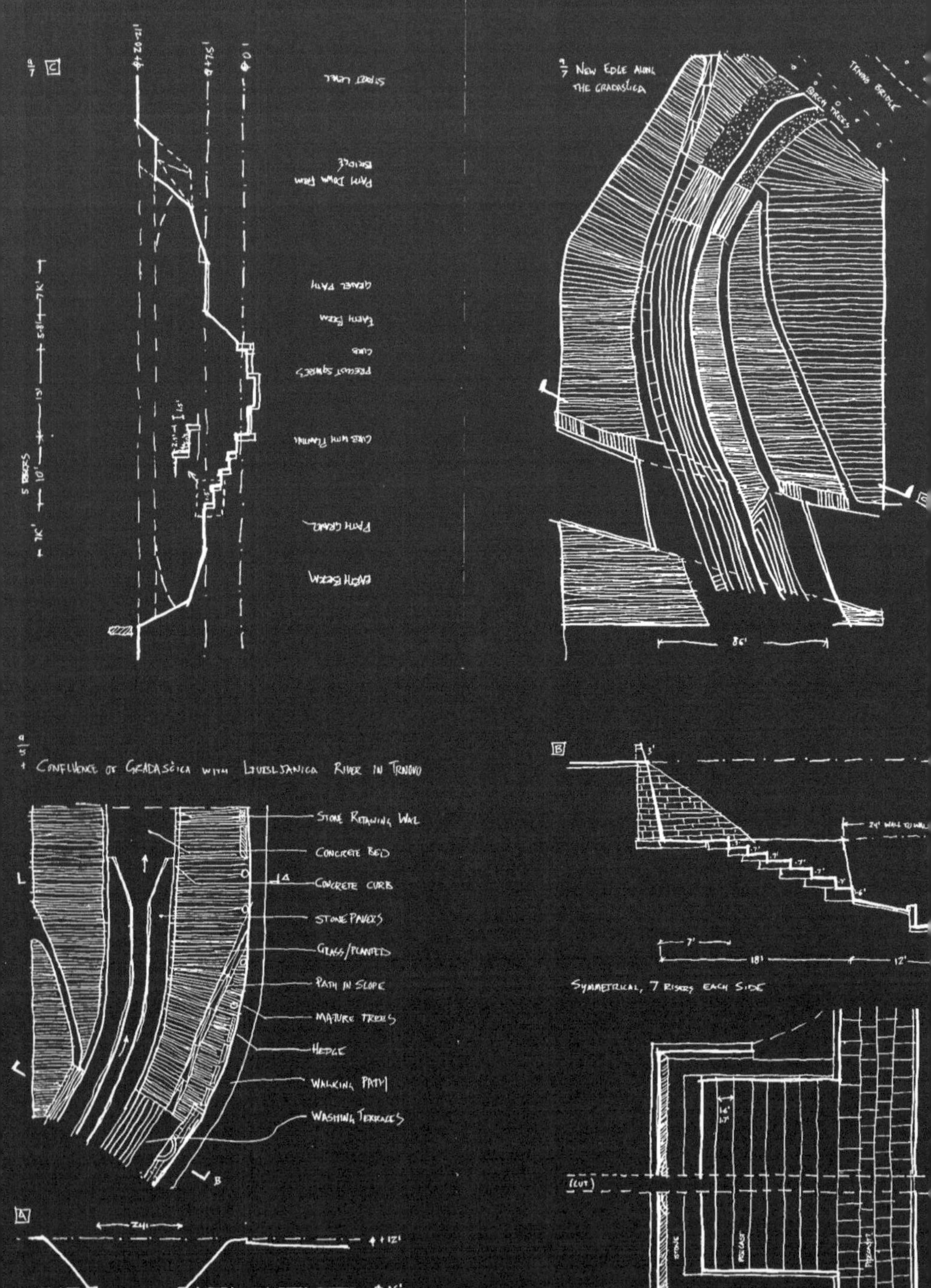
9/7 NEW EDGE ALONG THE GRADAŠČICA
CONFLUENCE OF GRADAŠČICA WITH LJUBLJANICA RIVER IN TRNOVO
STONE RETAINING WALL
CONCRETE BED
CONCRETE CURB
STONE PAVERS
GRASS/PLANTED
PATH IN SLOPE
MATURE TREES
HEDGE
WALKING PATH
WASHING TERRACES
SYMMETRICAL, 7 RISERS EACH SIDE
(CUT)

Jože Plečnik's infrastructural interventions along the Ljubljanica and Gradaščica rivers in Ljubljana, Slovenia represent a built encyclopedia of design strategies for leveraging the spatial characteristics and functional demands of water to produce a continuously varied and fantastically dynamic urban experience at the interface of the river and the city.

Funded by the Architectural League of New York Deborah D. Norden Fund award, I traveled to Ljubljana in September 2014 to study this two-and-a-half mile sequence of public works. I spent two weeks developing sketch drawings based on measured sectional conditions as I followed the two rivers from a rural condition to the city center and back out

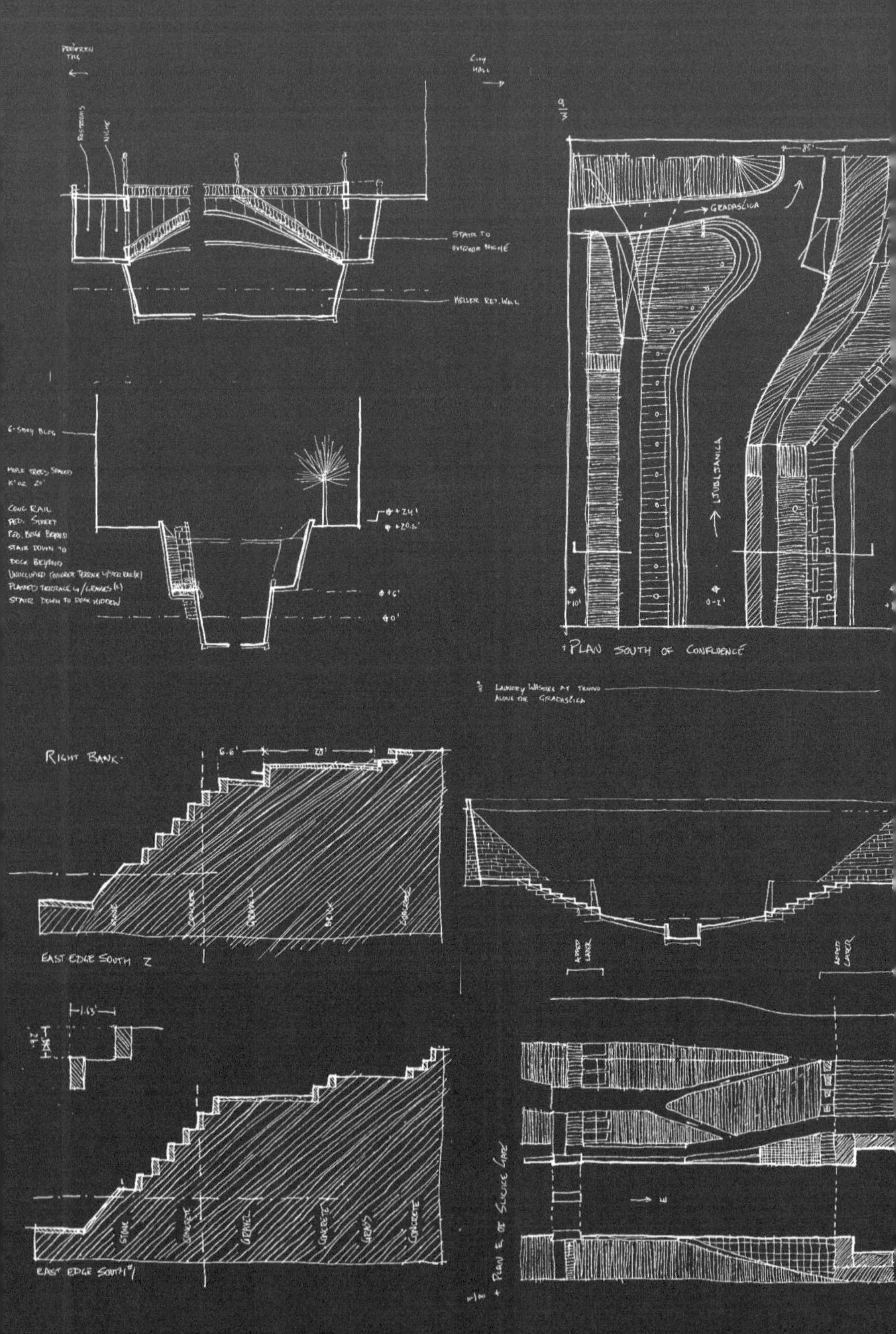

PREŠEREN TRG
RESTAURANT
NICHE
STAIR TO OUTDOOR NICHE
KELLER RET. WALL
CITY HALL
9/3
85'
GRADAŠČICA
LJUBLJANICA
+10'
0-2'
PLAN SOUTH OF CONFLUENCE
LAUNDRY WASHING AT TRNOVO ALONG THE GRADAŠČICA
6-STORY BLDG
MAPLE TREES SPACED 15' OR 20'
CONC. RAIL
PED. STREET
PED. BRIDGE BEYOND
STAIR DOWN TO
DOCK BEYOND
UNOCCUPIED (CONCRETE TERRACE W/STEEL RAIL(R)
PLANTED TERRACE W/LINDENS (L)
STAIR DOWN TO DOCK HIDDEN
+ 24'
+ 20.5'
+ 6'
0'
RIGHT BANK
6.6'
20'
EAST EDGE SOUTH Z
1.63'
2'
EAST EDGE SOUTH "I
PLAN E. OF SLUICE GATE

to the countryside, while simultaneously mapping the contextual, topographical, and situational provocations of the adjacent neighborhoods. Plečnik's designs - visionary at the time - anticipated a performatively resilient and programmatically rich approach to designing the edge of water.

Water continuously redefines its own edge. Since the beginnings of maritime trade, designers and city planners have been tasked with developing methodologies to establish a more predictable definition of this edge to allow for continued economic vitality and to ensure public safety. Advances after the industrial revolution resulted in engineered solutions to water management often biased toward achieving hard-edged regulation of this boundary to allow for unmitigated access to ports, docks, and coastlines for trade. Twenty-first century cities are faced with an abundance of inherited infrastructures that are monuments to outmoded design approaches, and the climate crisis has further catalyzed the need to consider a new definition - pliant rather than

BANKS OF THE LJUBLJANICA: 1765, 1915

prescriptive - for defining the limits, boundaries, and thresholds of water in the city.

The relationship of any city to its water is implicitly fraught with a paradoxical complication: it's necessary both to provide access to, and separation from, a volatile, shifting edge. During the first half of the 20th century, Jože Plečnik delivered a sequence of forward-thinking infrastructural projects executed in Slovenia - sectionally-unique approaches to designing the flow of the river Ljubljanica through the nation's capital Ljubljana, which had in the past had a symbiotic relationship with the water but was prone to severe flooding.

Brimming with symbolic ornamentation and historical reference, Plečnik's

LEFT: PEGLEZEN, 1932 - 1934
RIGHT: NATIONAL AND UNIVERSITY LIBRARY, 1936 - 1940

architectural work during the first half of the twentieth century was seemingly out-of-step with the prevailing social and cultural imperatives of early modernism. His interest in the vernacular imagery of native Slovenia (then Yugoslavia) and idiosyncratic building style were later sources of reference for early postmodernists. Surveys of his work published during this period largely overlook Plečnik's large-scale but formally restrained public works executed over the course of decades in parallel with his stylistically-exuberant architectural projects [1].

Ironically, Plečnik's inhabitable sections and multi-functional, programmatically rich infrastructural systems - not dissimilar in concept from megastruturally-scaled

EXCERPT OF PLEČNIK'S 1943 REGULATION PLAN FOR LJUBLJANA
SHOWING EXISTING AND PROPOSED CONNECTIONS

armatures like Le Corbusier's Plan Obus for Algiers or Kenzo Tange's Tokyo Bay - demonstrate a synchronicity with the visions of his contemporaries.

In the early 1930's Plečnik, in collaboration with the city's public works department, rapidly developed plans for the revitalization of two rivers which traverse the urban core of Ljubljana. These plans were part of a larger effort by Plečnik to modernize Ljubljana by identifying key areas - arterial roads, squares, and bridges - in need of renovation. In the inter-war period he was the de facto architect of the city, and was able to execute large-scale urban improvements by working closely with the municipal engineer Matko Prelovšek, translating conceptual sketch drawings into built work at a rapid pace. [2]

CONSTRUCTION OF CONCRETE EMBANKMENTS ALONG THE LJUBLJANICA

The river project itself was a bit of deferred maintenance after a 19th century dredging project, and by the time Plečnik initiated his involvement, municipal engineers had already developed a plan to install a concrete embankment. The beginnings of his work saw him proposing flourishes to the engineered plan; eventually he became more deeply involved in coordinating the design of the edge. Plečnik worked to identify strategies - linkages, occupiable thresholds, engineered walls, and soft edges - that could incorporate or accommodate the inevitable cycles of flooding all while redefining space around the waters' edge to provide open access for citizens.[2]

Plečnik's solutions constitute an experiential infrastructure, where a minimally-constructed site serves

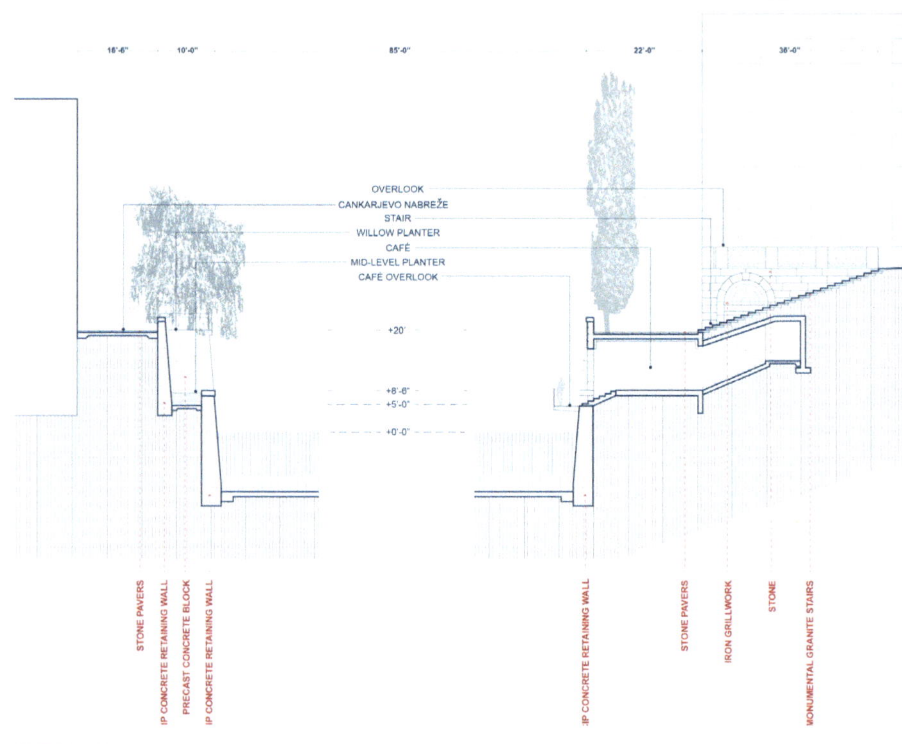

SECTION OF THE LJUBLJANICA NEAR KONGRESNI TRG

as a neutral element against which measurements of the landscape with respect to time, history, distance, and the water may be made. His designs leverage the latent potential of under-utilized sites into zones for pedagogy and phenomenological experience. Through the lens of new cultural and ecological imperatives, engineers, architects, landscape architects, ecologists, and urban planners have been charged with understanding how spatial and material variations in the vertical section affect the primarily horizontal behavior of water: Jože Plečnik's projects demonstrate methodologies that capture the spatial, programmatic, and viscerally experiential nature of waterfront sites even as they address the pragmatic and quantitative requirements of water management.

The Ljubljanica, the larger of the two rivers, cuts across the grain of the city in its center. Along the Ljubljanica, the design of the river embankments is closely synced with the relative level of density of adjacent neighborhoods.

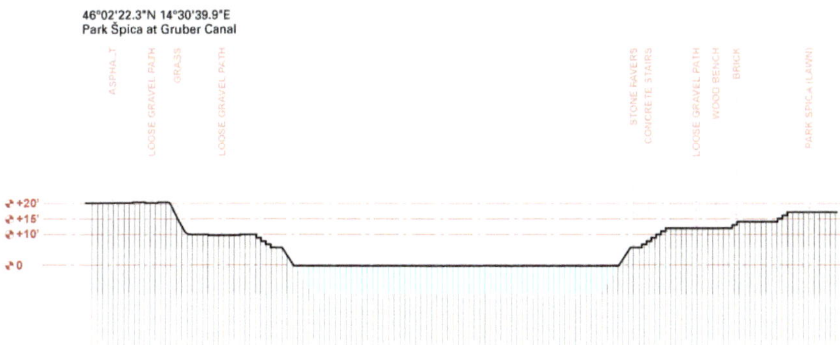

At the suburban southern end of the city, the river is depressed fifteen to twenty feet from the adjacent grade and the banks take the character of a shaded promenade or linear park with descending paths and shortcut stairs for pedestrian access at intersections. Immediately adjacent to the water, a highly articulated, stepped stone edge provides terraced seating and

demarcates the relative height of the river. Sloping, planted berms provide sectional separation and reinforce the idea of an outdoor room within the city.

Plečnik's landscape design - most notable

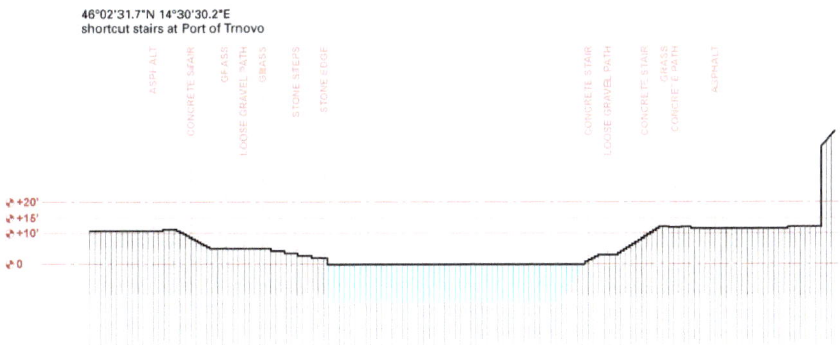

here for its linear arrangement of willow trees - acts to frame the space in these rooms and to delineate distinct precincts.

Further north, in the city center, the embankments are constructed as a high, hard-edged channel. Here, the section develops a more overtly architectural character, where inhabitable indoor and

outdoor spaces at an intermediate level are carved out of an otherwise monolithic infrastructure. Simultaneously a series of lush terraced landscape planters built into the embankment support giant poplars and a lushly planted landscape.

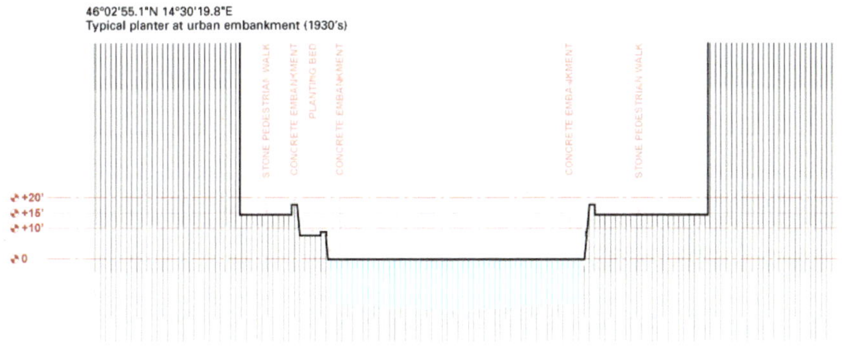

Plečnik first began working on the waterfront in the late 1920's with a series of elaborate bridge projects, most notably at Tromostovje (Triple Bridge), an expansion of a vital crossing that linked the medieval historic city to an emerging modern business district. Plečnik's primary bridges, all nearly as wide as they are long, function as urban plazas,

reclaiming area in the densest parts of the city for commerce, promenade, and performance. Where the Triple Bridge meets Plečnik's Central Market project (1940's), the notion of a ground plane is subverted completely as stairs to an

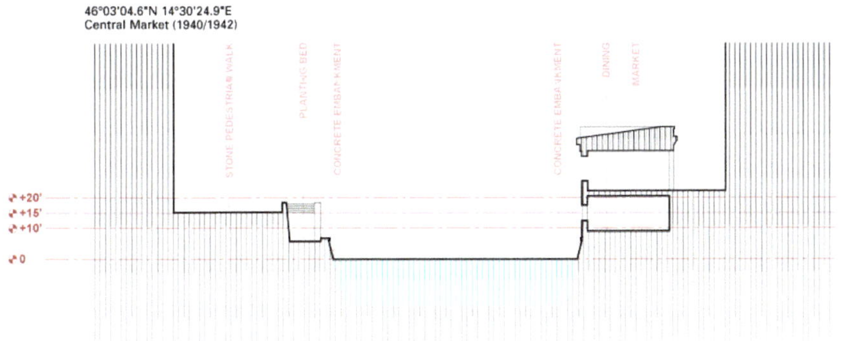

intermediate level fold down from the pedestrian footbridge to give access to a new lower mezzanine. Here at the city center, the multi-level market, both indoor and outdoor, is itself the embankment.

At the eastern edge of the city, high concrete embankments give way to a

hybrid concrete-and-berm approach, culminating in Plečnik's monumental Sluice Gate. Miles out, the Ljubljanica re-exerts itself as a low, wide, meandering river.

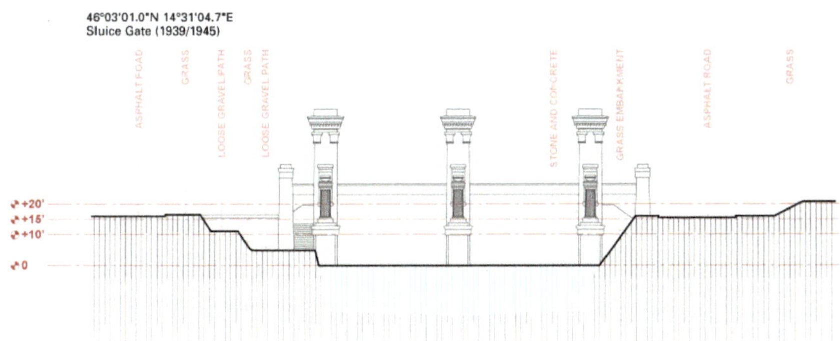

Plečnik's interventions in the city are experienced as a narrative sequence, where distances are linked by visual markers, large-scale iconography gives meter to a walkable city, and widened or

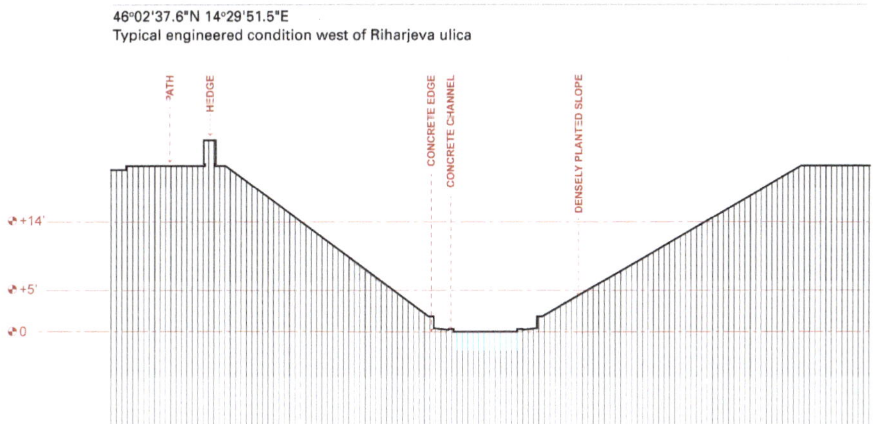

otherwise distinguished ground planes create new primary corridors. Nowhere is this more true than along the Gradaščica, which flows west-to-east and empties into the Ljubljanica. As it enters the city from the west, the river flows in a symmetrical channeled condition into the Trnovo district where steeply sloping banks are

retained by a concrete wall and the river banks themselves are laid with stone

Over the deep crevice of the Gradaščica, Plečnik designed a new crossing – the iconic Trnovo bridge – marking the

46°02'36.2"N 14°30'07.8"E
Trnovo Bridge (1932)

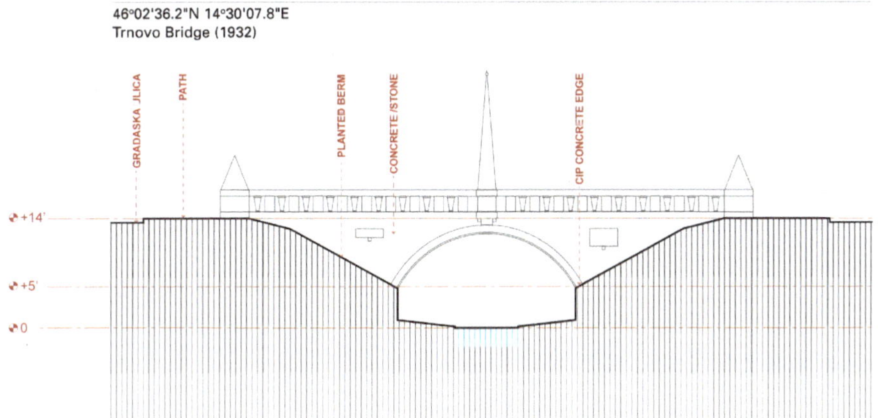

entry to the district. The bridge is a wide planted platform, itself an extension of the urban grade.

In Trnovo, a primarily residential suburb, Plečnik introduced steeply sloping paths in the bermed earth to give access down to the water, and at the edge, a shallowly sloping bank accommodates seasonal

storm surges. Further east, Plečnik inserted a retaining wall and a series of wide steps as laundry washing terraces. Today this zone, with its densely shaded tiered seating, is informally repurposed

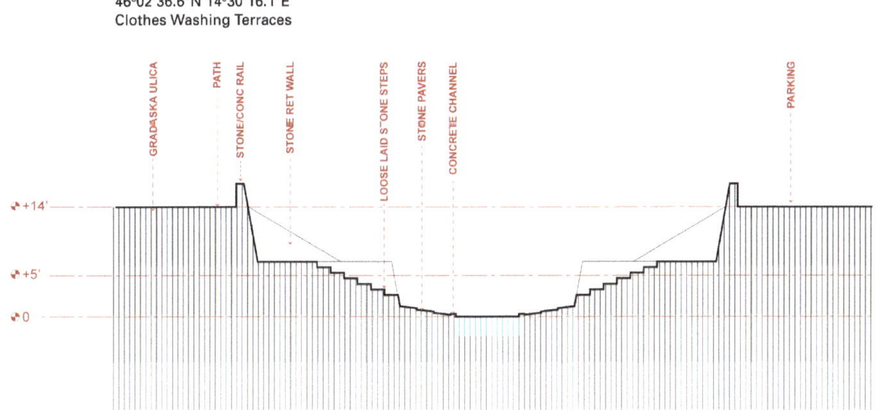

for leisure. Further down the Gradaščica, the river widens into a vertically-walled concrete channel and empties into the Ljubljanica at the Port of Trnovo.

Along the Ljubljanica and Gradaščica, the built-up character of the river embankments themselves is synced with the relative level of urbanity and density of adjacent neighborhoods. The river acts as an organizing and orienting element in the city, where access and exit points to the river promenade are calibrated to the cross-grain of the neighborhood streets. The river projects constitute a linear park but the system is clearly calibrated to operate transversely, connecting adjacent neighborhoods and binding otherwise bifurcated precincts along a meandering central spine.

In his master plan and in the construction of the embankments, Plečnik identified locations for future bridge connections, and in the time since, beginning in the 1950's and continuing through to

Gradaščica 5 - Trnovo Bridge

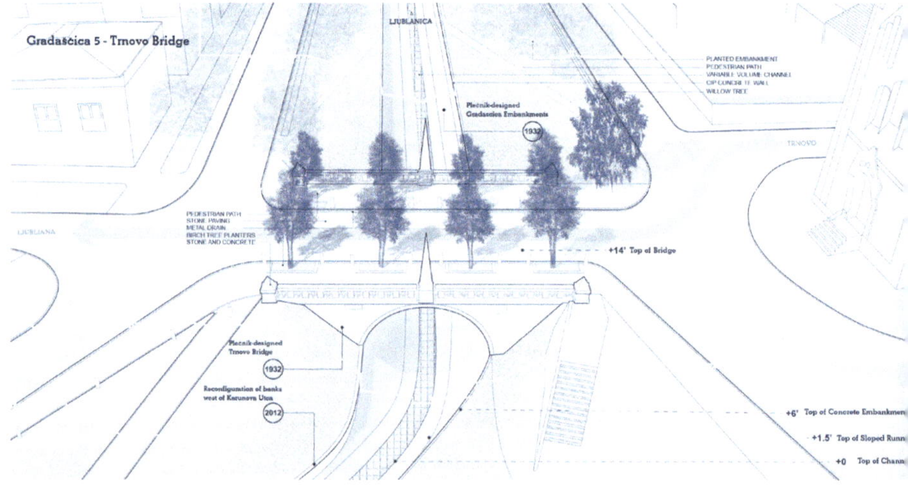

TRNOVO BRIDGE IS A BROAD CONCRETE PLATFORM CLAD IN STONE AND DENSELY PLANTED WITH BIRCH TREES. THE BRIDGE EXTENDS THE GROUND PLANE AND LOCALLY CAPS THE GRADAŠČICA TO CREATE A NEW PUBLIC SPACE ON AXIS WITH A THE HISTORIC CHURCH OF JOHN THE BAPTIST.

the present, designers have continued to develop the embankment projects. Plečnik's approach to designing the edge sets up an open-endedness that both accommodates future developments and suggests a sectional vocabulary for their implementation which has now been taken up by a newer generation of Slovenian designers: the embankments along both rivers continue to evolve today.

There is little in his archives to suggest that Plečnik had a progressive ecological agenda, but his pragmatic design approach was one that inherently addressed not only the operative requirements of these systems to contain, control, and deliver the water through the city but their ability to contribute to civic life in the capital. Given the performative mandate of water management in surge-prone cities and

HARD-SOFT GRADIENT OF EDGE CONDITIONS ALONG THE LJUBLJANICA

the seemingly paradoxical trend toward
waterfront urbanism, his work at the rivers
in Ljubljana, long neglected, is now more
relevant than ever. Mega-scale projects by

their nature alter their contexts; the most
effective infrastructures are those that
are multivalent and can activate further
transformations that enhance urban life.

Index of Conditions

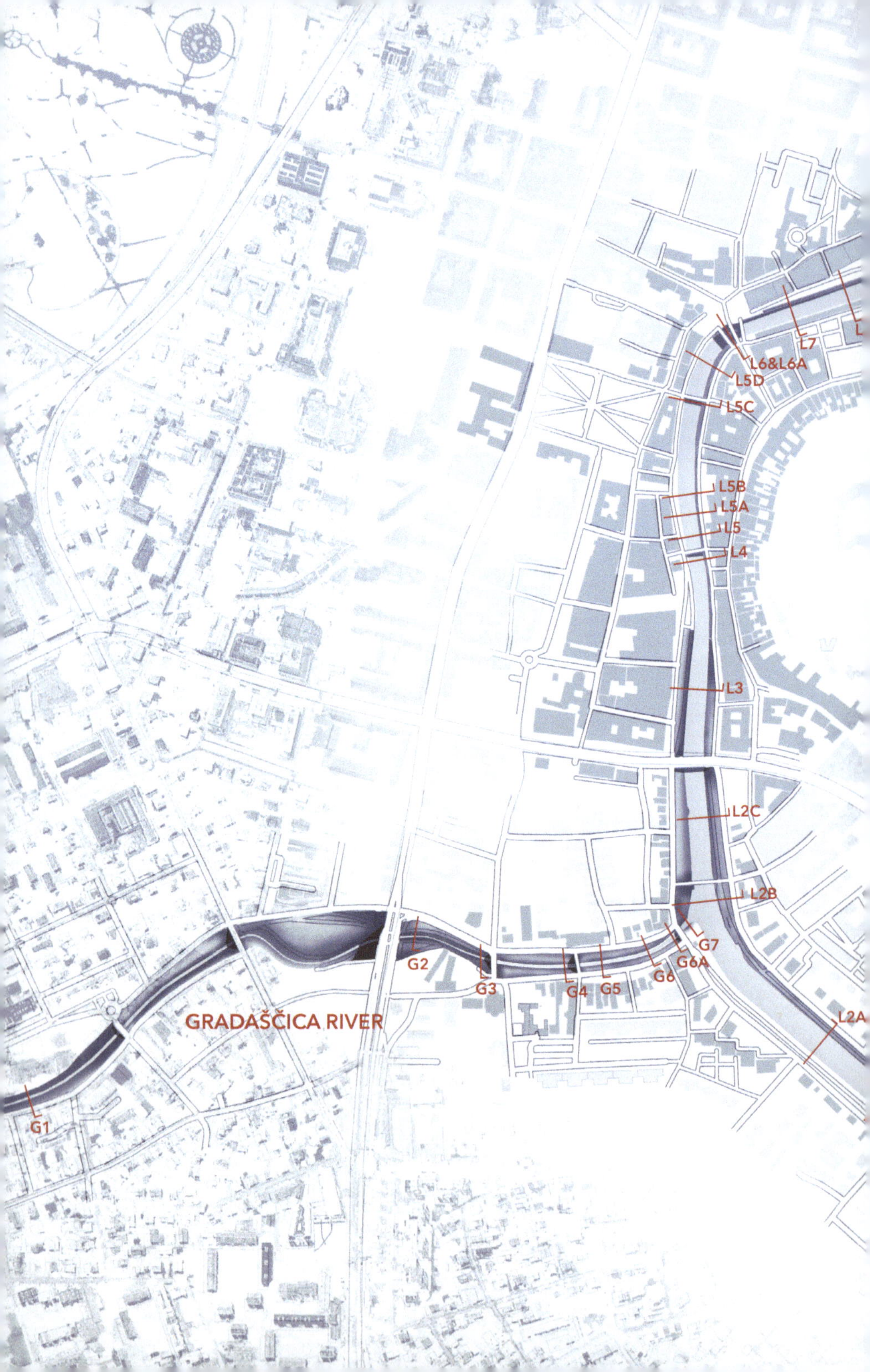

L7
L6&L6A
L5D
L5C
L5B
L5A
L5
L4
L3
L2C
L2B
G7
G6A
G6
G5
G4
G3
G2
G1
L2A
GRADAŠČICA RIVER

L8
LJUBLJANICA RIVER
L9
1C
L1B
L1A
L1

Gradaščica 1

46°02'37.6"N 14°29'51.5"E
Typical engineered condition west of Riharjeva ulica

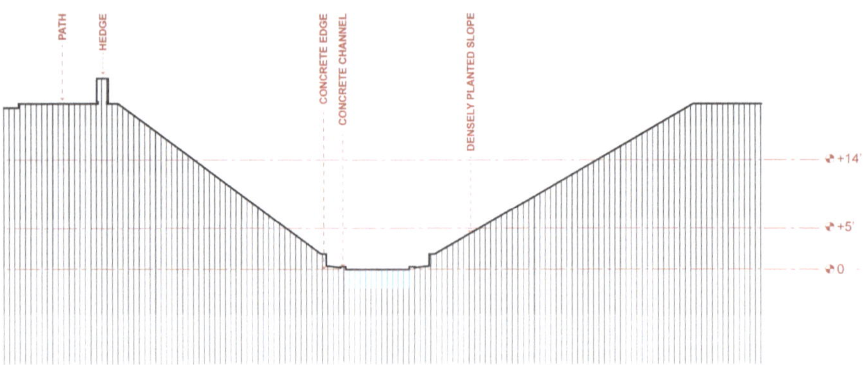

Gradaščica 2

46°02'37.5"N 14°30'03.4"E
2012 Rearrangement, URBI

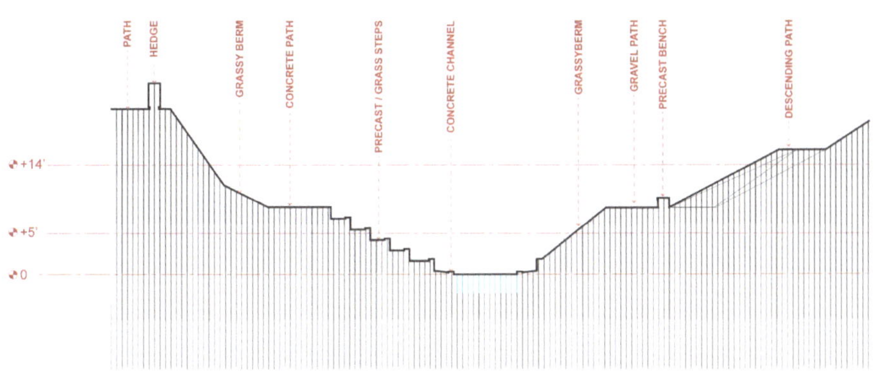

Gradaščica 3

46°02'36.2"N 14°30'07.8"E
Trnovo Bridge (1932)

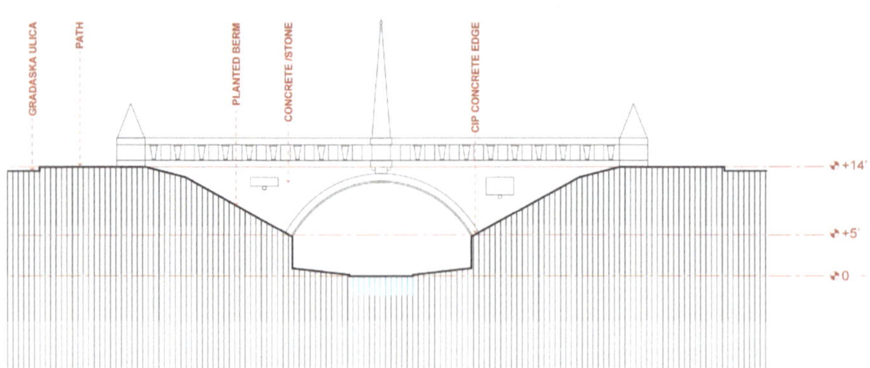

Gradaščica 4

46°02'36.4"N 14°30'13.1"E
Petelinja brv (Rooster) Footbridge (1931)

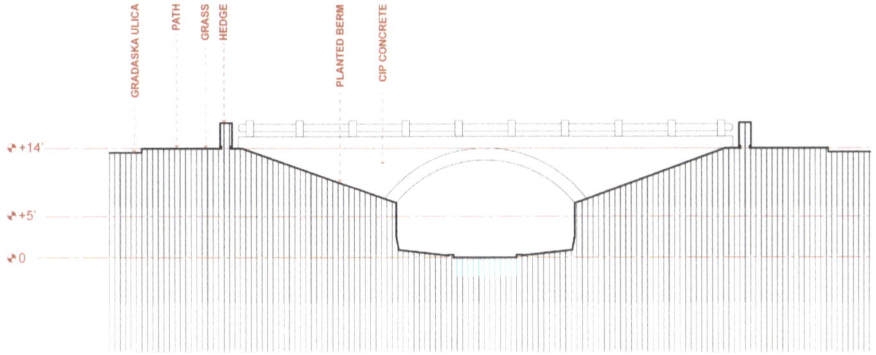

Gradaščica 5

46°02'36.6"N 14°30'16.1"E
Clothes Washing Terraces

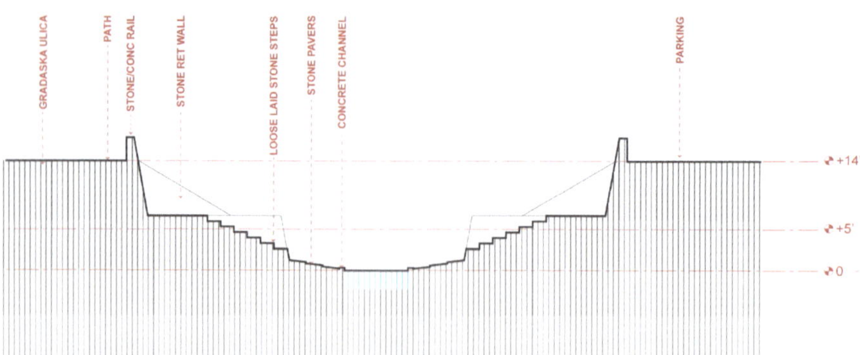

Gradaščica 6

46°02'36.9"N 14°30'17.5"E
Pedestrian path integrated in landscape edge

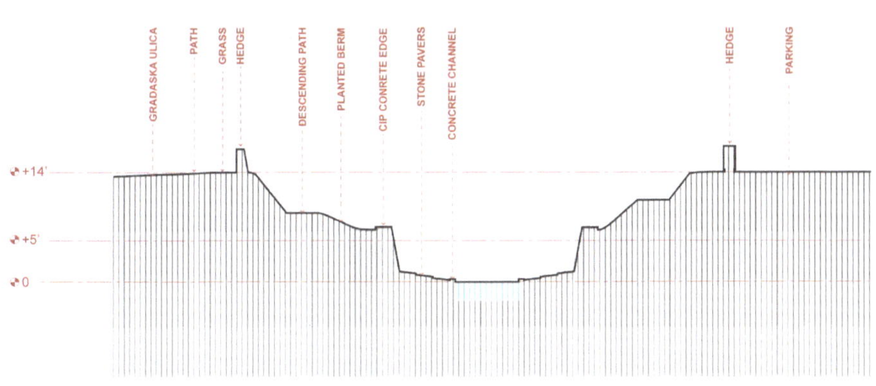

Gradaščica 6a

46º02'37.2"N 14º30'18.7"E

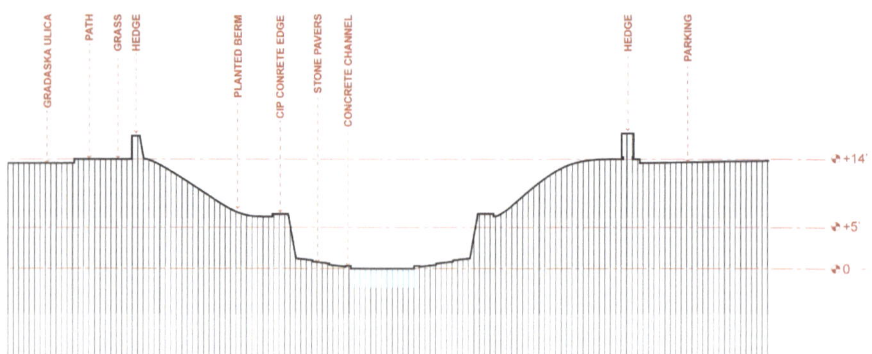

GRADASKA ULICA
PATH
GRASS
HEDGE
PLANTED BERM
CIP CONRETE EDGE
STONE PAVERS
CONCRETE CHANNEL
HEDGE
PARKING
+14'
+5'
0

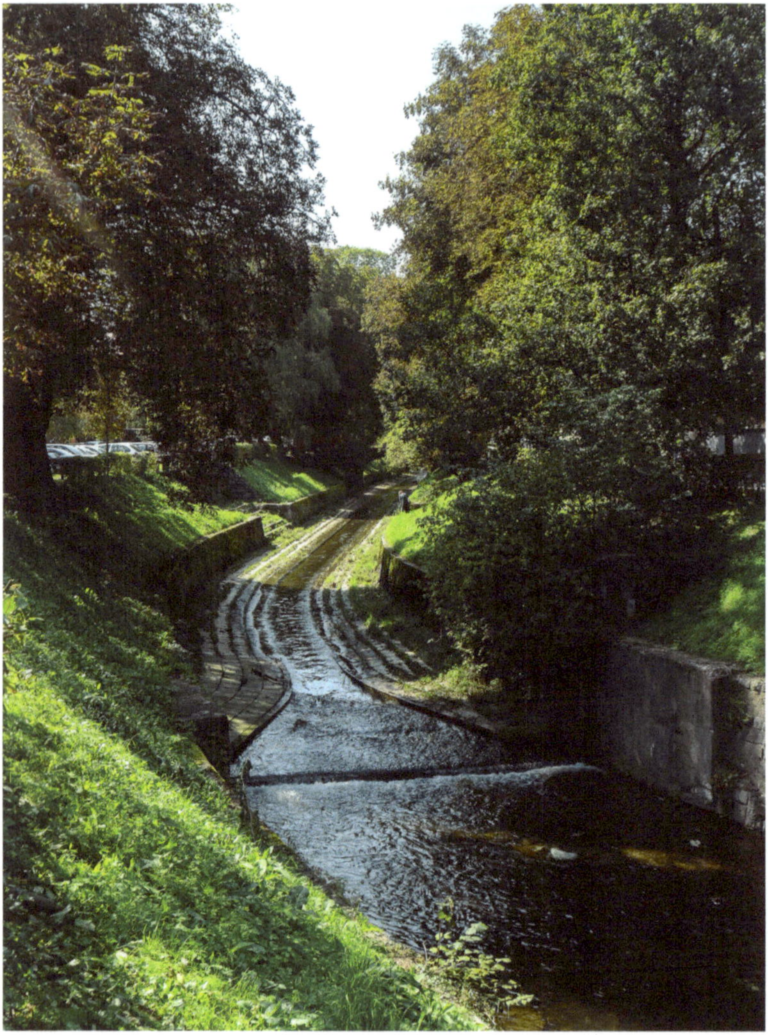

Gradaščica 7

46°02'37.9"N 14°30'21.6"E
Confluence with the Ljubljanica River at the Jek Bridge

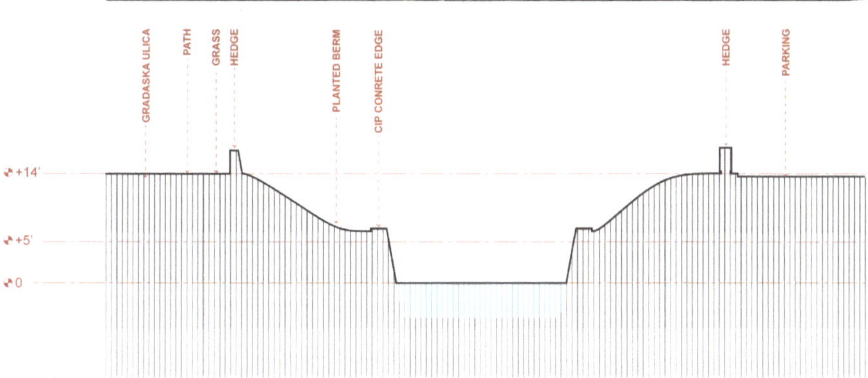

Ljubljanica 1

46°02'22.3"N 14°30'39.9"E
Park Špica at Gruber Canal

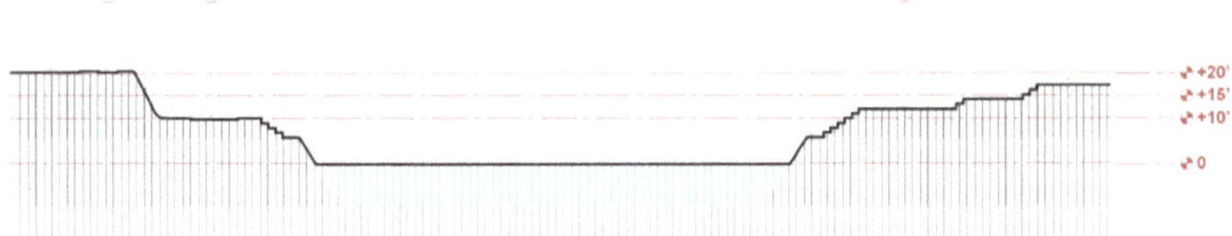

Ljubljanica 1a

46°02'23.9"N 14°30'39.6"E
Park Špica with recent enhancements (2011)

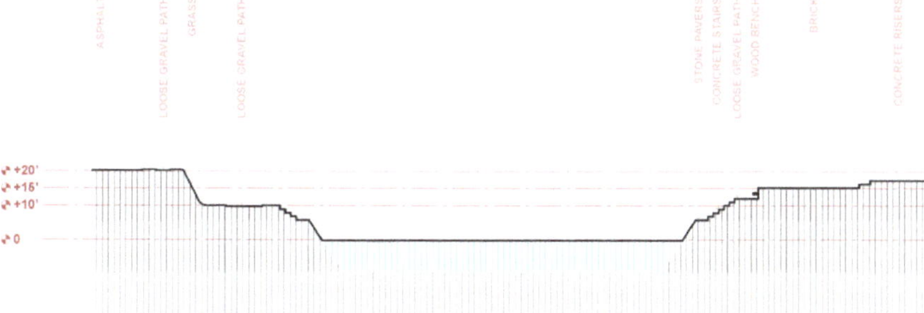

Ljubljanica 1b

46°02'26.2"N 14°30'37.7"E
Park Barge at Privoz (2012)

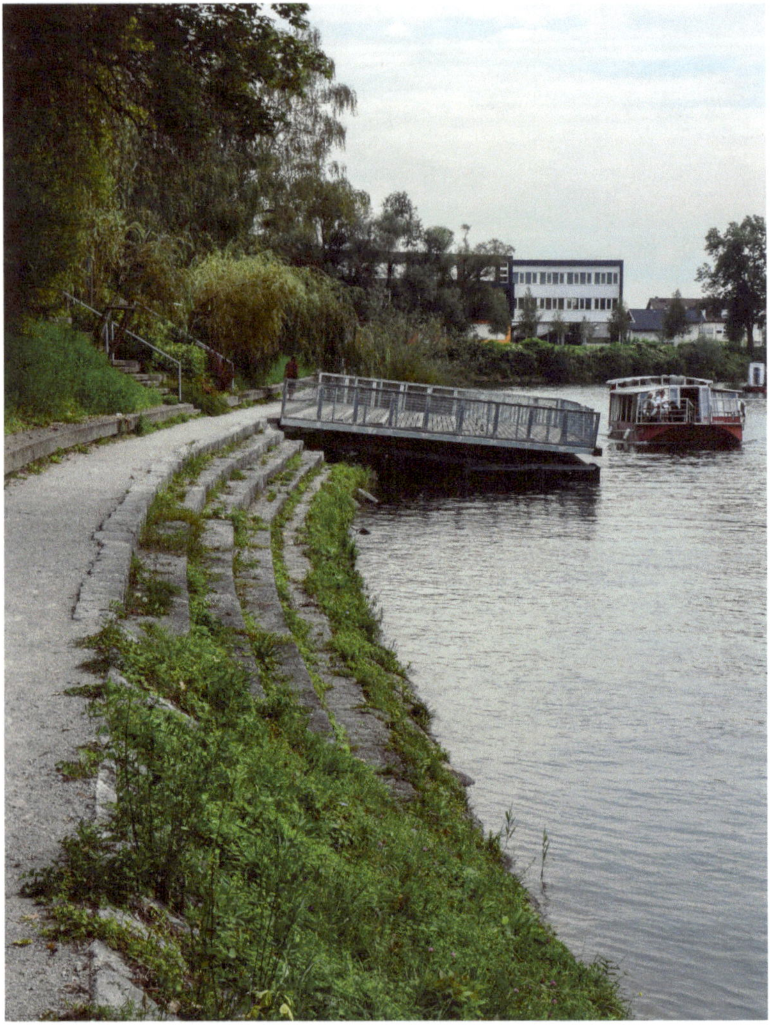

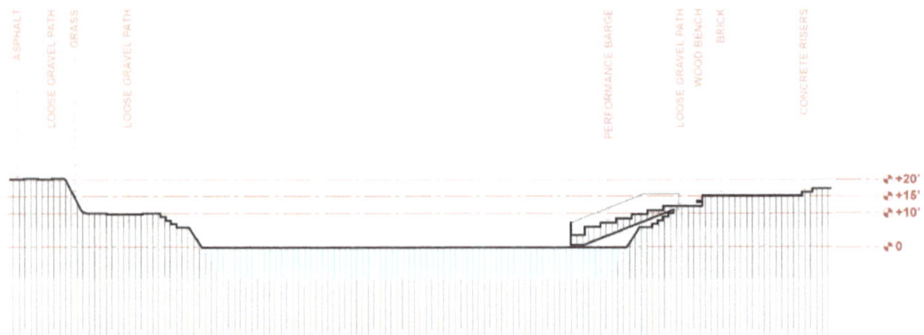

Ljubljanica 1c

46°02'26.9"N 14°30'37.1"E

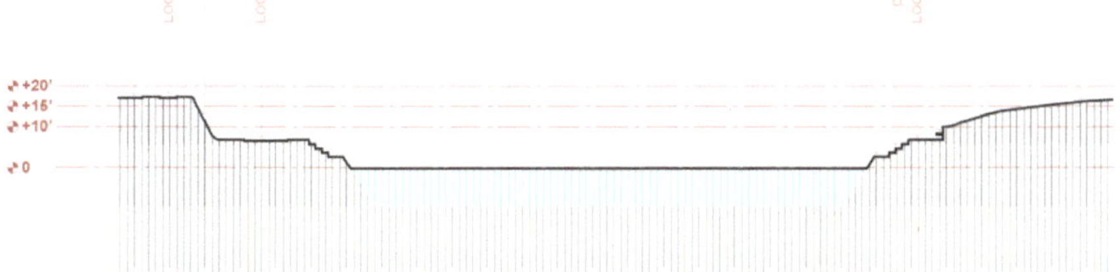

Ljubljanica 1d

46°02'28.9"N 14°30'34.9"E
near Janežičeva cesta

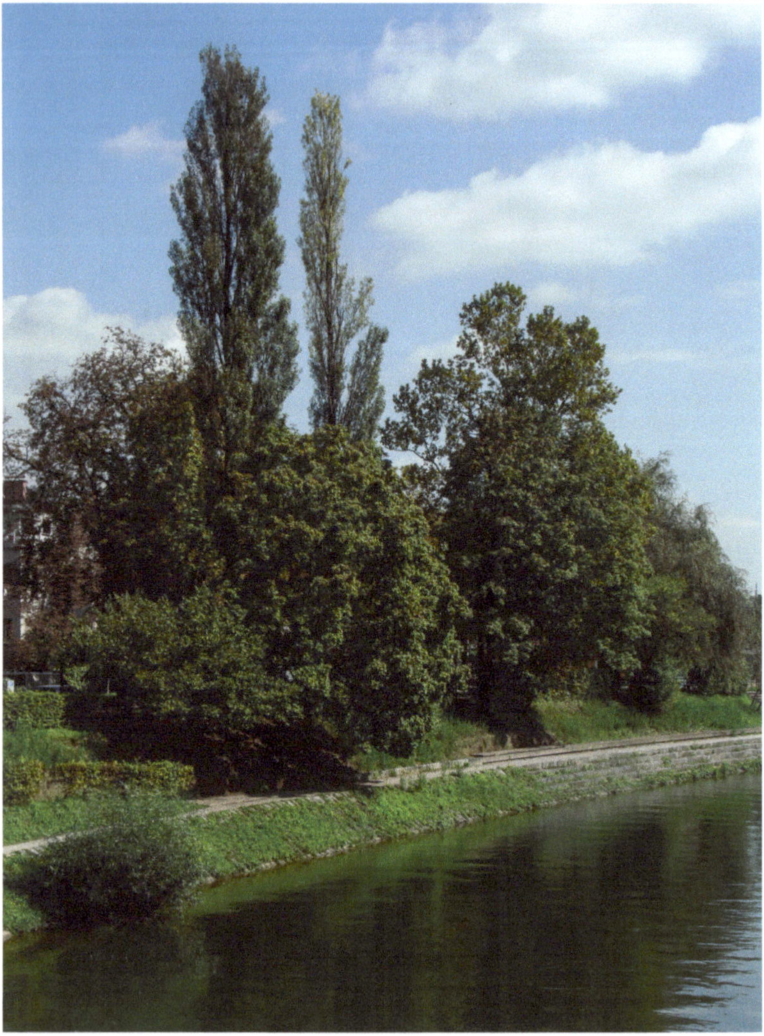

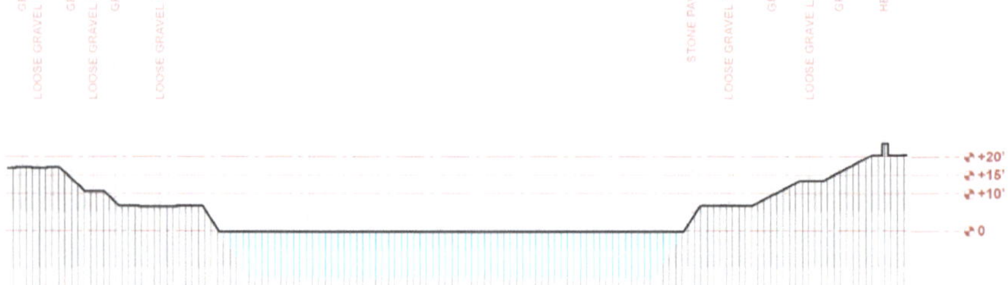

Ljubljanica 2

46°02'30.8"N 14°30'31.6"E
Port of Trnovo

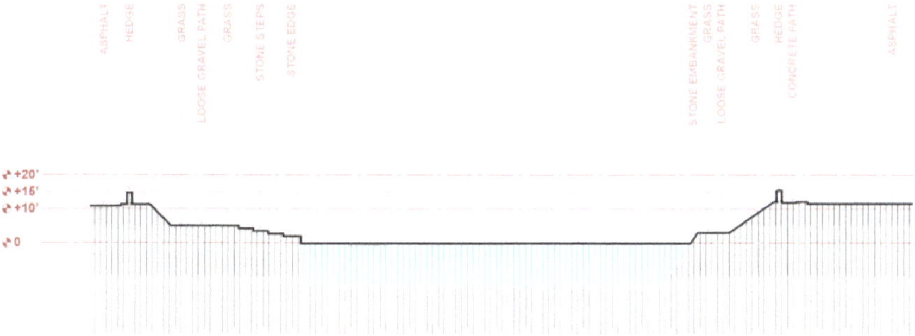

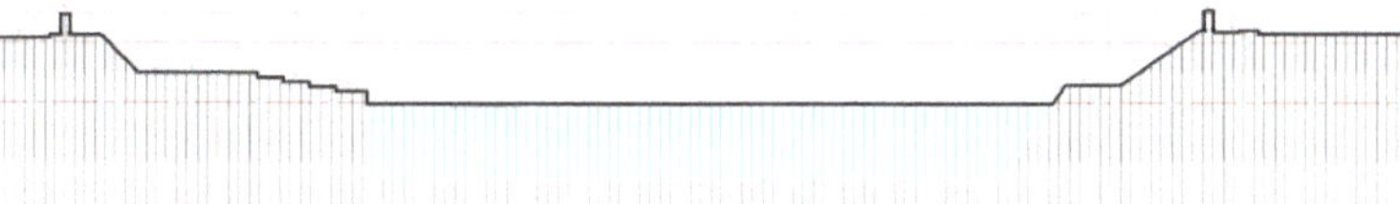

Ljubljanica 2a

46°02'31.7"N 14°30'30.2"E
shortcut stairs at Port of Trnovo

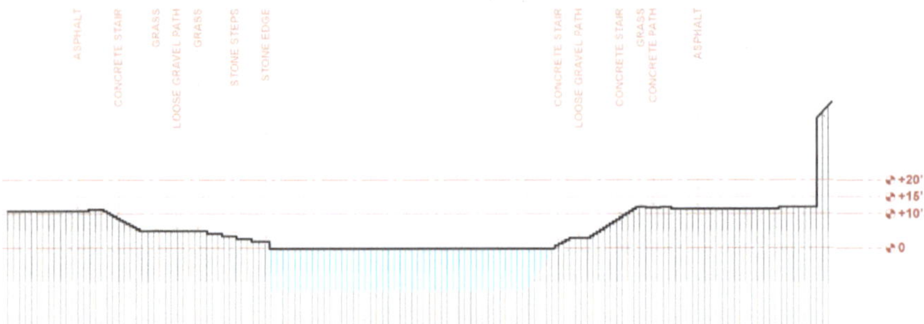

Ljubljanica 2b

46°02'37.9"N 14°30'21.4"E
Port of Trnovo (1930) with boat launch

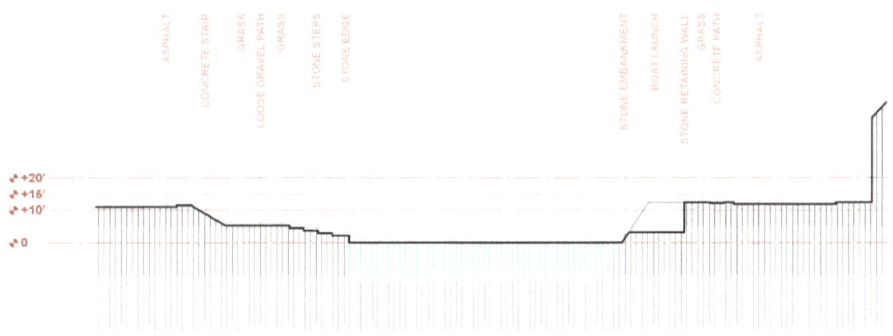

Ljubljanica 2c

46°02'39.6"N 14°30'20.6"E
Renovated right bank (2012)

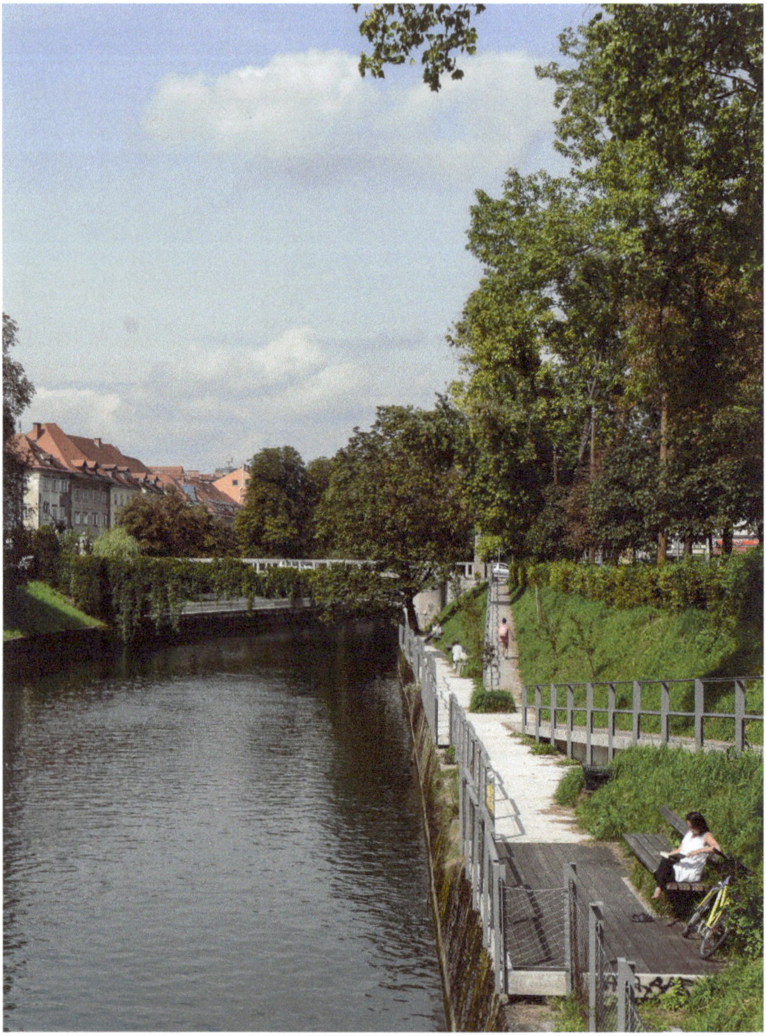

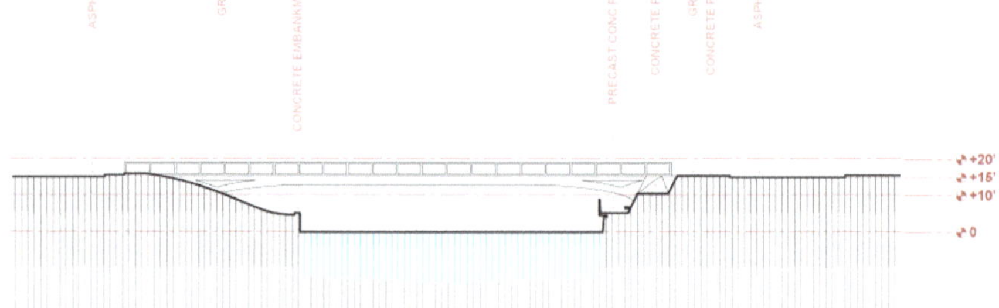

Ljubljanica 3

46°02'46.4"N 14°30'20.2"E

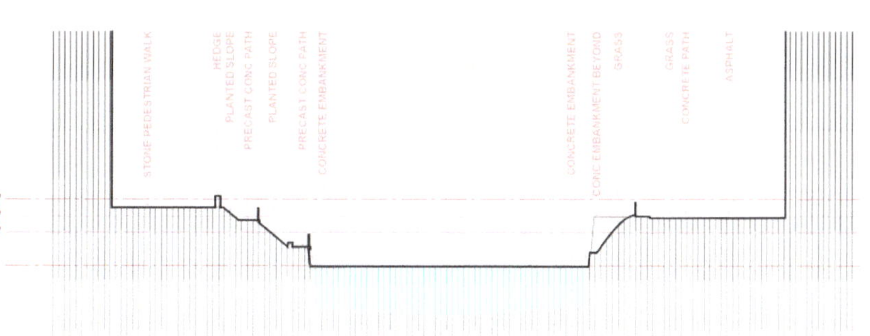

STONE PEDESTRIAN WALK
HEDGE
PLANTED SLOPE
PRECAST CONC PATH
PLANTED SLOPE
PRECAST CONC PATH
CONCRETE EMBANKMENT
CONCRETE EMBANKMENT
CONC EMBANKMENT BEYOND
GRASS
GRASS
CONCRETE PATH
ASPHALT
+20'
+15'
+10'
0

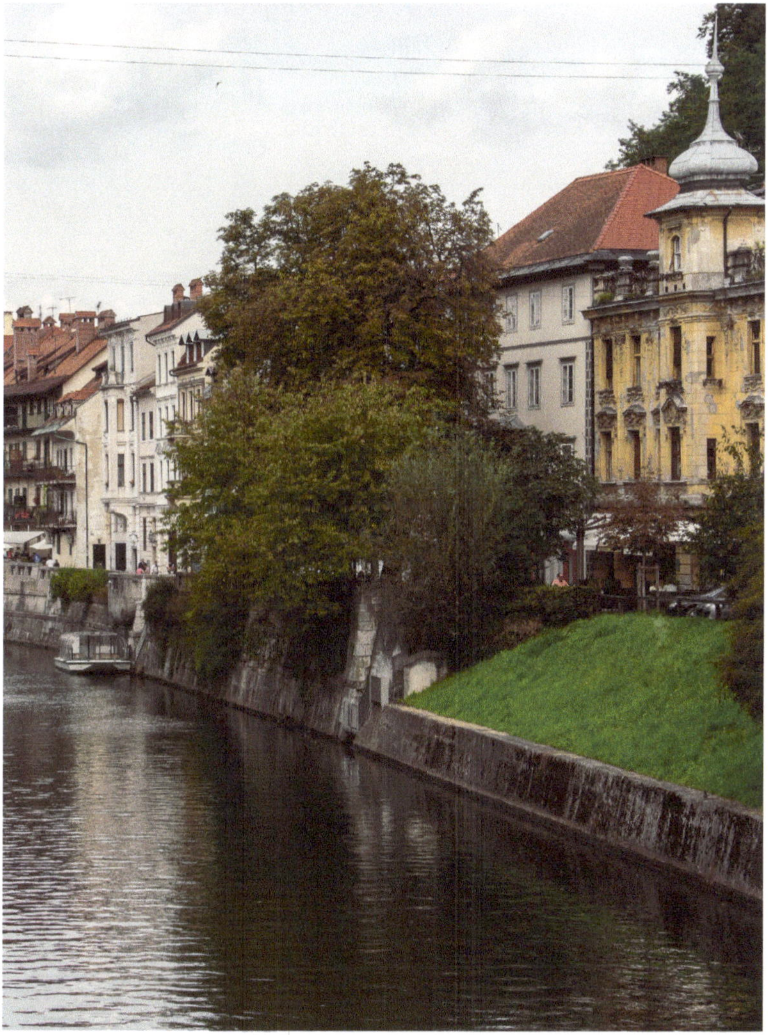

Ljubljanica 4

46°02'54.0"N 14°30'20.2"E
Čevljarski most (1932)

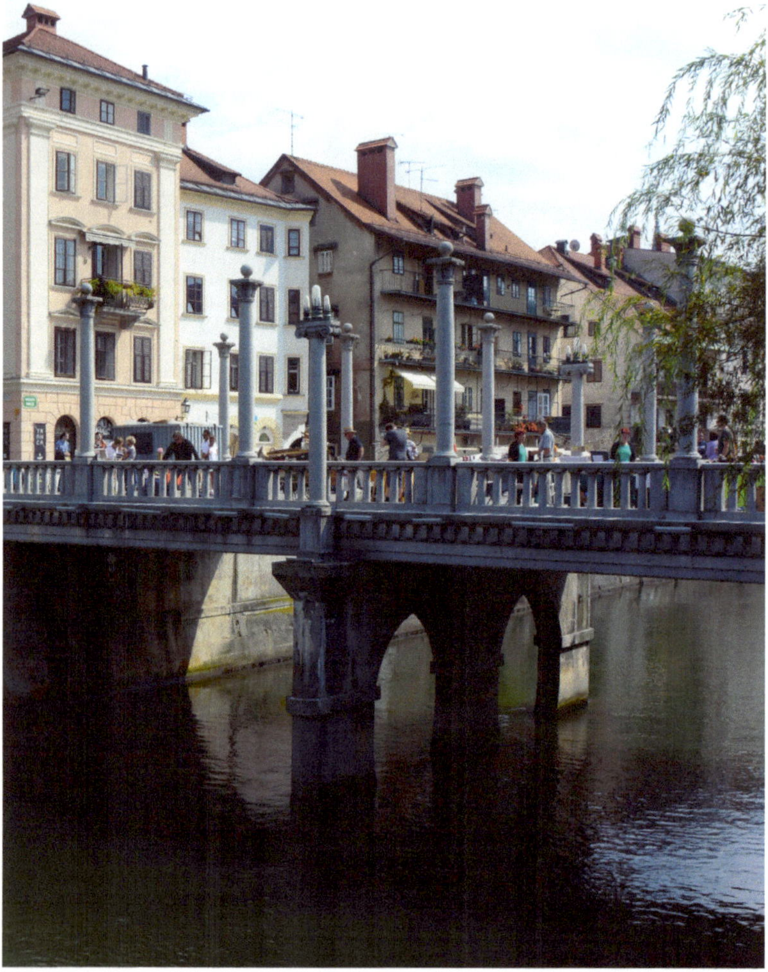

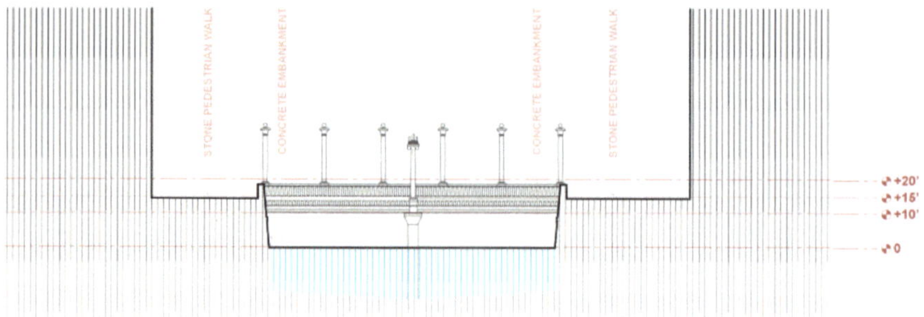

Ljubljanica 5

46°02'55.1"N 14°30'19.8"E
Typical planter at urban embankment (1930's)

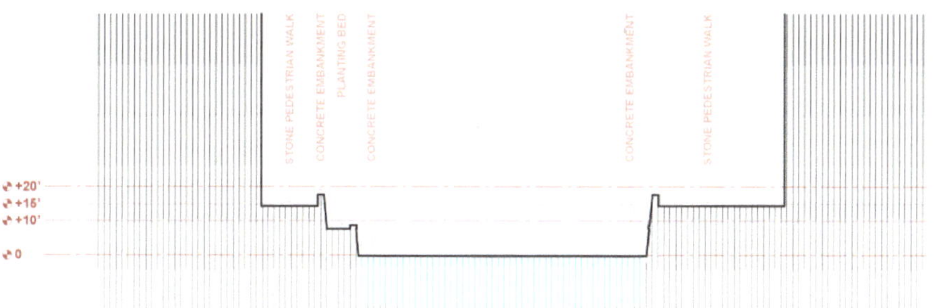

Ljubljanica 5a

46°02'56.1"N 14°30'19.7"E
Typical urban embankment (1930's)

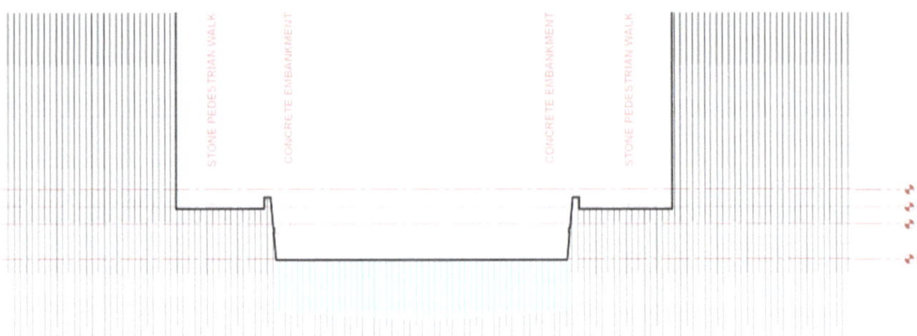

Ljubljanica 5b

46°02'56.9"N 14°30'19.5"E
Embankment Stair at Dvorni Trg

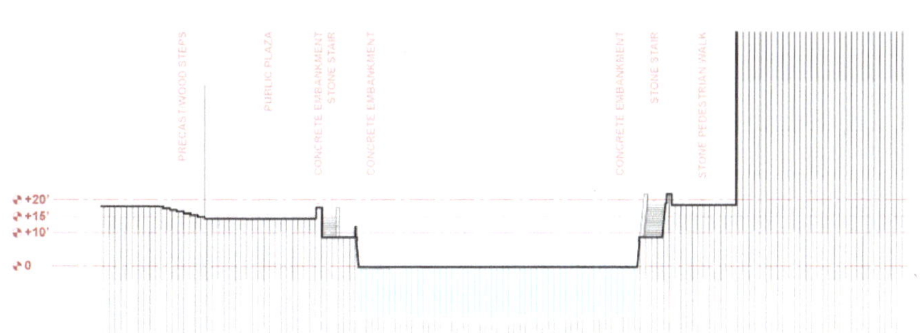

Ljubljanica 5c

46°03'01.1"N 14°30'19.9"E
Gerber's Staircase (1933) with Footbridge by Arhitektura d.o.o. (2012)

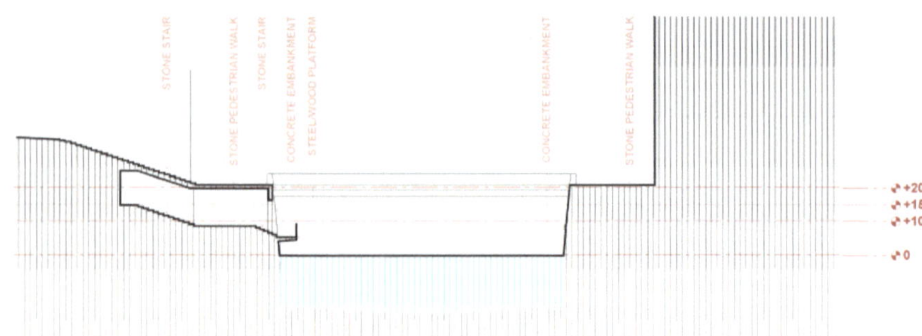

Ljubljanica 5d

46°03'02.6"N 14°30'20.7"E
Terraced cafe and planters near Triple Bridge

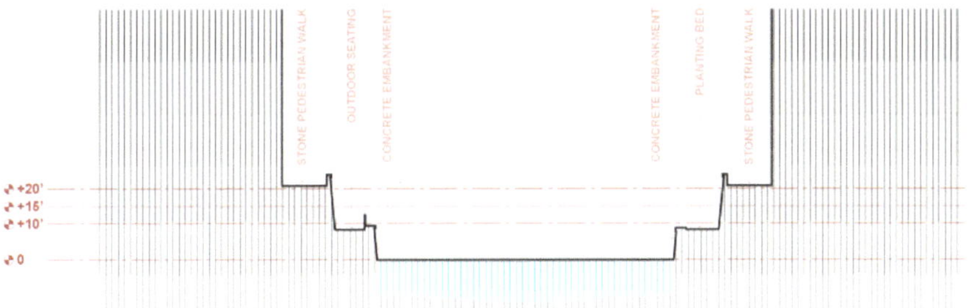

Ljubljanica 6

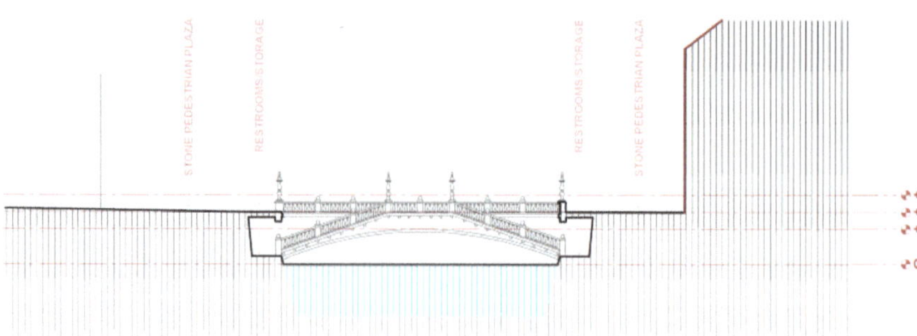

Ljubljanica 6a

46°03'03.7"N 14°30'21.8"E
Triple Bridge (1932)

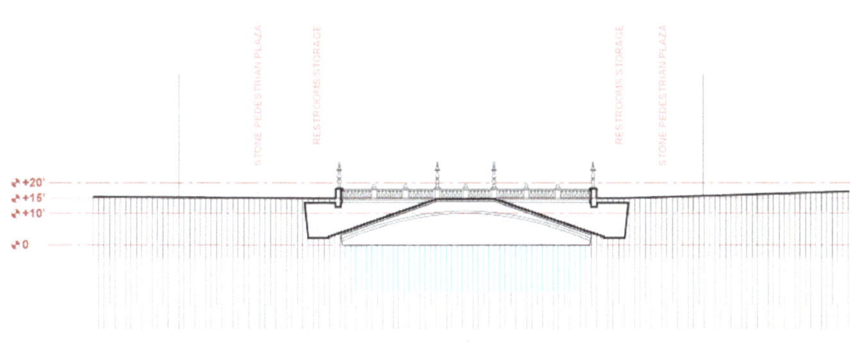

Ljubljanica 7

46°03'04.6"N 14°30'24.9"E
Central Market (1940/1942)

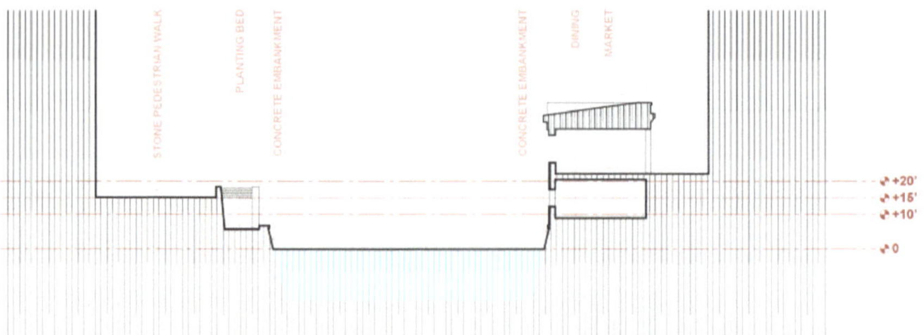

STONE PEDESTRIAN WALK
PLANTING BED
CONCRETE EMBANKMENT
CONCRETE EMBANKMENT
DINING
MARKET
+20'
+15'
+10'
0

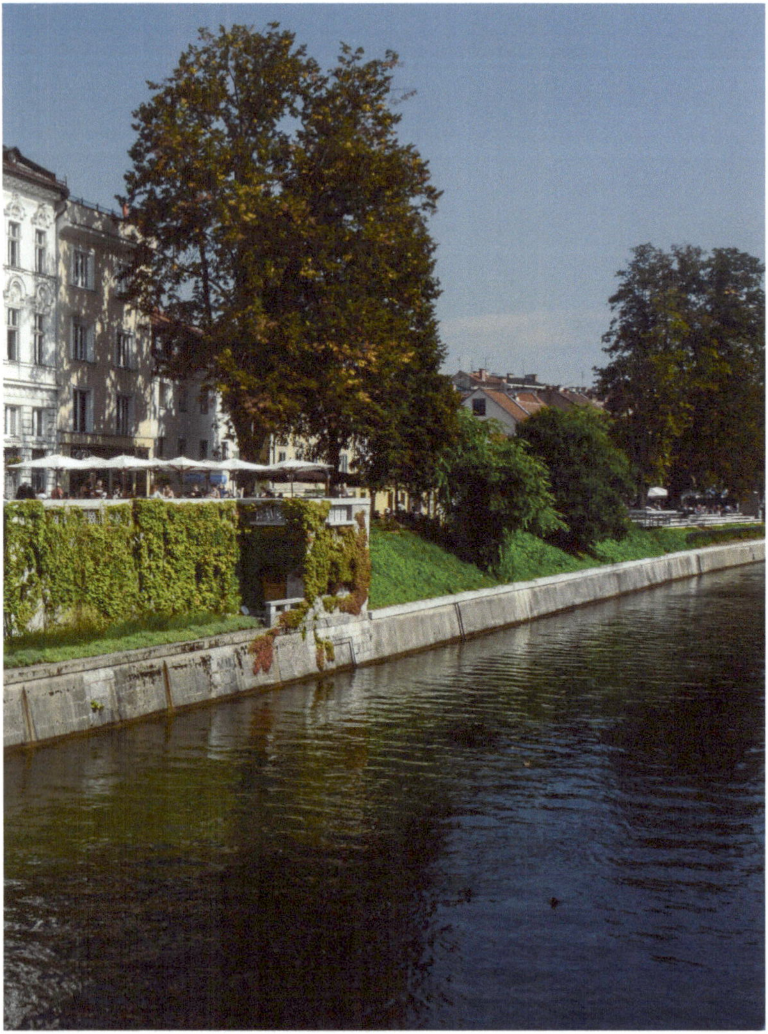

Ljubljanica 7a

46°03'05.5"N 14°30'28.7"E
Central Market (1940/1942)

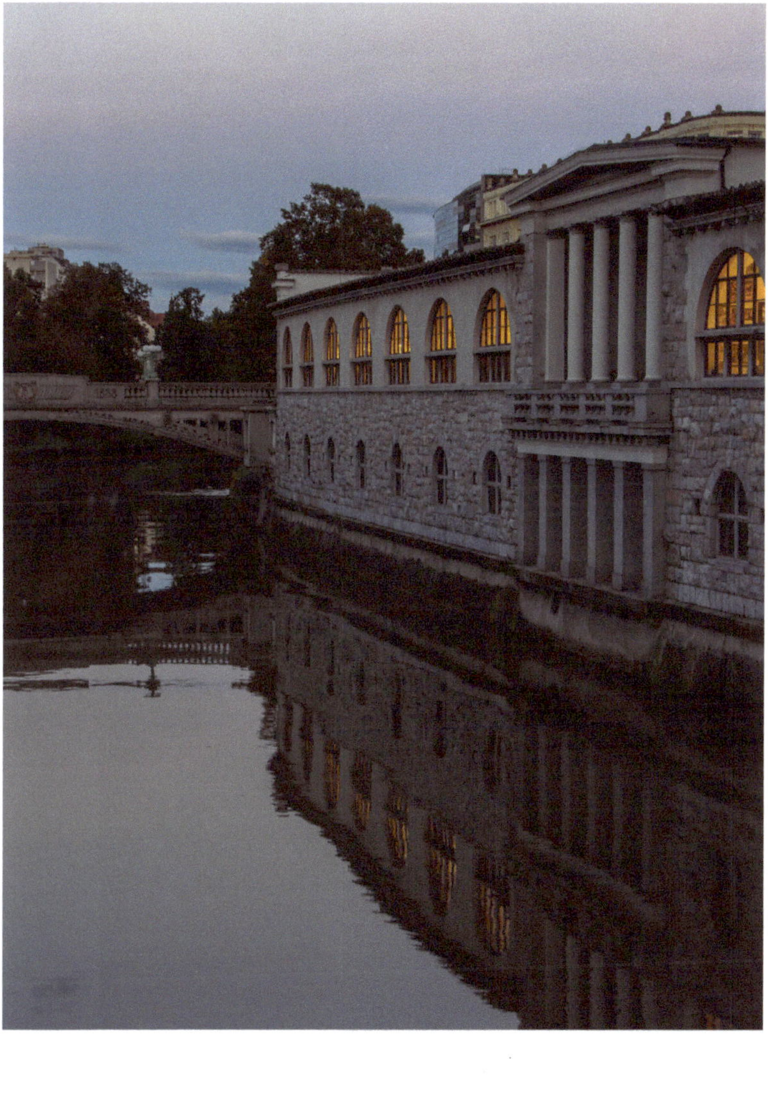

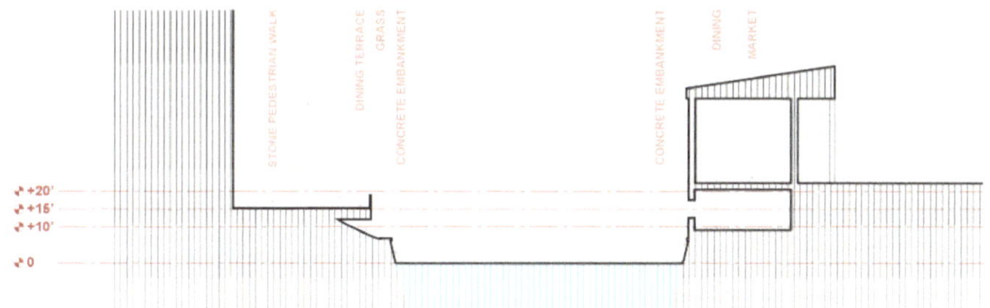

Ljubljanica 8

46°03'06.8"N 14°30'43.6"E
Typical Embankment from Dragon Bridge to Žitni most

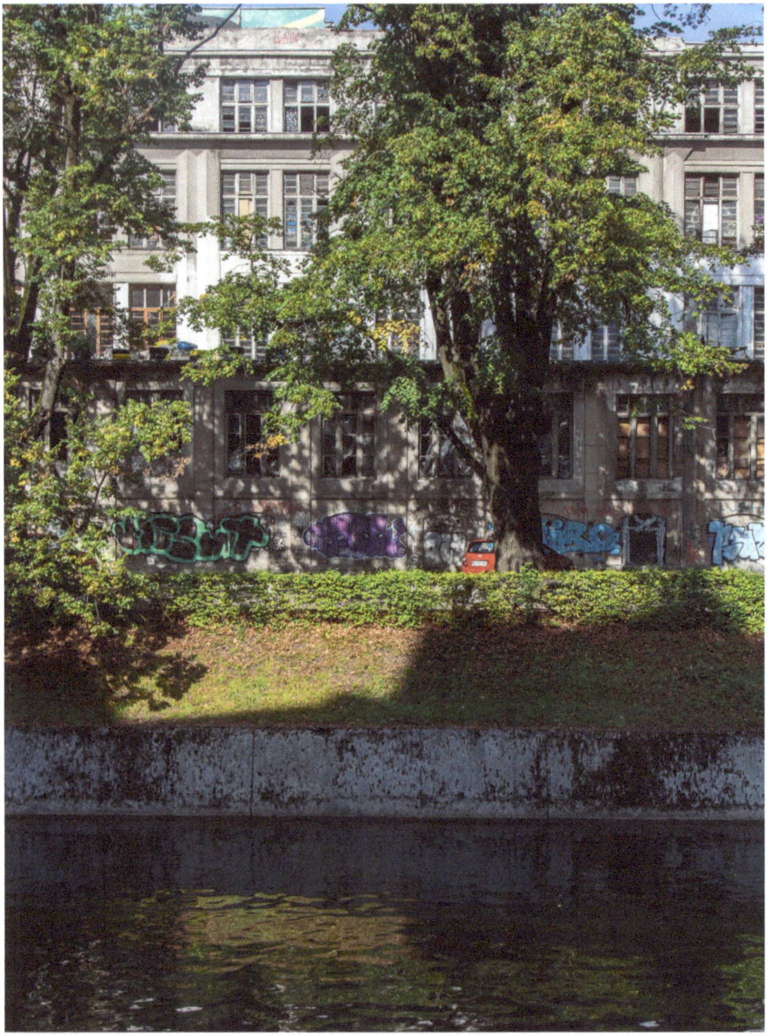

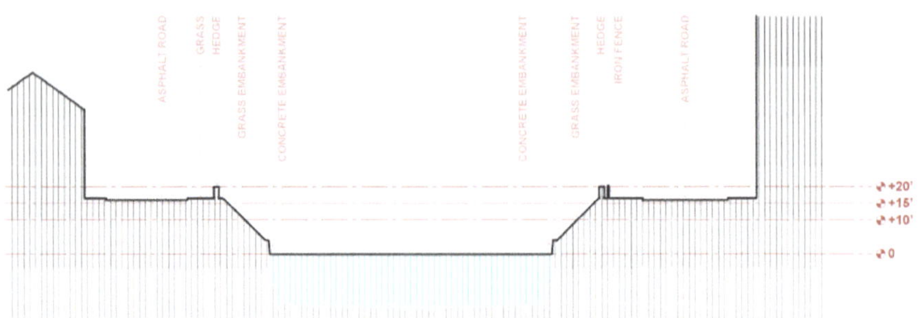

Ljubljanica 9

46°03'01.0"N 14°31'04.7"E
Sluice Gate (1939/1945)

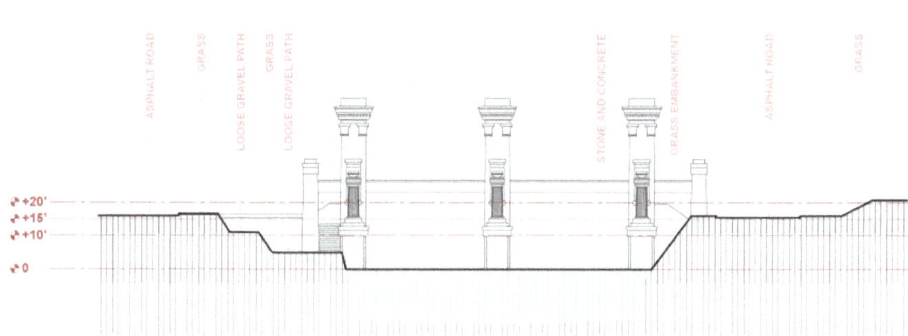

ASPHALT ROAD
GRASS
LOOSE GRAVEL PATH
GRASS
LOOSE GRAVEL PATH
STONE AND CONCRETE
GRASS EMBANKMENT
ASPHALT ROAD
GRASS
+20'
+15'
+10'
0

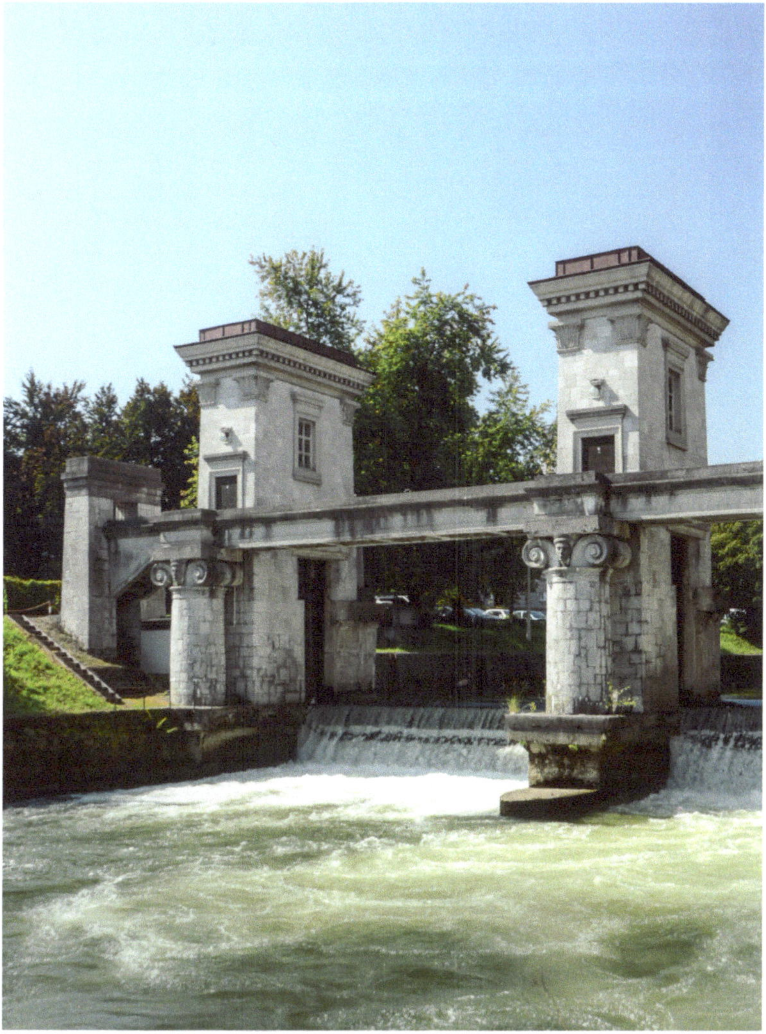

Plečnik Projects: Mapping the Embankments Along the Gradaščica and Ljubljanica is the product of travel research funded by the 2014 Deborah D. Norden Fund Prize awarded by the Architectural League of New York.

Image Credits:
P10: Historic Images and postcards in public domain
P14: Site plan courtesy of MGML
P16: Construction photos by Peter Naglič, images used with permission of Matjaž Šporar
All other photography and drawings by Kerry O'Connor

Notes:

1. Burkhardt, François. et. al., editors. *Jože Plečnik, Architect 1872 - 1957*. MIT Press, 1989.
2. Krečič, Peter. Plečnik: *The Complete Works*. Whitney Library of Design, 1993.